Contents

Introduction

The charming castle at Hever, situated in the heart of idyllic countryside, has a rich and varied history dating back more than 700 years. Yet much of what visitors see today is the result of the remarkable efforts of a wealthy American, William Waldorf Astor, who used his fortune to restore and extend the Castle in the early 20th century, and to assemble its magnificent collection of antique portraits, furniture and tapestries.

The picturesque castle at Hever formed the unlikely backdrop to a sequence of tumultuous events that changed the course of Britain's history, monarchy and religion. The original medieval defensive castle with its gatehouse and walled bailey was built here in 1270 and, in the 15th and 16th centuries, was the home of one of the most powerful families in the country, the Bullens, who added the Tudor dwelling within the walls. The Castle was to become the childhood home of Hever's most famous inhabitant, Anne Boleyn, King Henry VIII's second wife, who became Queen of England for just 1,000 days. It was Henry's love for Anne and her insistence that she became his wife rather than remain his mistress that led to the King renouncing Catholicism and creating the Church of England.

Hever Castle later passed into the ownership of another of Henry VIII's wives, Anne of Cleves, and from 1557 onwards it was owned by a number of families including the Waldegraves, the Humphreys and the Meade Waldos. Gradually, it fell into decline but in 1903 William Waldorf Astor invested vast amounts of time, money and imagination into restoring the Castle, building the adjoining Tudor Village, now called the 'Astor Wing' and constructing the magnificent gardens and lake. At Hever, his wealth and vision enabled him to create a lavish family home that also indulged his passion for history.

❝ There is a place very dear to my family and me not far from where we live. We come to it in all weathers, all seasons, and this is where we recharge our batteries: Hever Castle. ❞

Dame Judi Dench

for the Visit Britain 'You're Invited' TV campaign broadcast around the world

Facing page: Hever Castle from across the moat.

The Castle

The Inner Hall

The splendour of the reception room that greets visitors to Hever today is a complete contrast to its original use in Tudor times, when this was the Great Kitchen, complete with a large fireplace for cooking and a well for water.

The panelling and richly carved columns are made of Italian walnut. The gallery above the hall was inspired by the screen in King's College Chapel, Cambridge, and was executed in 1905 by W.S. Frith as part of William Waldorf Astor's restoration of 1903–08. The chandelier suspended from the ornate ceiling is 20th-century silver; a copy of an 18th-century design from an original at Knole House in Kent.

The Inner Hall now houses a fine collection of antique furniture, which dates mostly from the 17th and 18th centuries, and many fine paintings. On the walls are portraits of three generations of Tudor monarchs: Henry VII, Henry VIII and Edward VI. The painting hanging to the left of the fireplace is of Anne Boleyn and, to the right, is her older sister, Mary. The oldest piece of furniture in the Inner Hall stands in the window bay. The walnut cassapanca, or marriage chest, dates from around 1550. It is the Tudor equivalent of a 'bottom drawer' and was used for storing garments, documents and valuables collected during an engagement, but it also doubled as a seat.

The clock on the mantelpiece is a 20th-century replica of Henry's wedding gift to Anne Boleyn. The original belonged to Horace Walpole in the 18th century. It was bought by the Keeper of the National Gallery for the Queen in the 20th century.

Above: 16th-century style Spanish warming table (detail).
Facing page: Mid 18th-century bronze statuette of Henry VIII.

Above: Silver-plated clock, *c.* 1900. A replica of Henry VIII's wedding gift to Anne Boleyn.

Above: Detail of andiron, *c.* 1890.

Top: The Inner Hall.
Above: Early 18th-century Aubusson tapestry.

Above: Detail of the ceiling.

The Drawing Room

The Drawing Room is one of the beautiful rooms created by William Waldorf Astor, who entertained his guests lavishly here, as did his descendants in later years. It was in this room that visitors would have been served drinks before dinner. The Astors were renowned for their hospitality. House party guest lists, correspondence and photographs show that they socialised with royalty, prime ministers and many famous people such as Queen Elizabeth II, Winston Churchill, Sir Arthur Conan Doyle, and George Bernard Shaw, to name but a few.

When designing and creating this room and, indeed, all the rooms in the Castle, Astor paid great attention to detail and insisted that his workmen used, as far as possible, the same materials and tools as Tudor and Elizabethan craftsmen. The fine panelling in the Drawing Room was inspired by the beautiful Elizabethan panelling at Sizergh Castle, Cumbria.

Astor managed to harmonize history with 20th-century convenience and comfort and there are several interesting items in this room that illustrate this success, including a semi-circular satinwood George III commode that has been converted to house a record player. There is also a Blüthner baby grand piano in rosewood satin finish (c. 1922), whilst the impressive carpet (c. 1890–1900) is from Eastern Turkestan and would have taken a large team of people around eight years to make.

With the exception of one duplicate, all of the beautiful panels in the elegant Drawing Room are different, and were made from oak, bog-oak and holly in 1905. One hides a secret door that leads to a turret – the Astor family hid the drinks cabinet in there!

Facing page: View of the Drawing Room with its Khotan carpet and fine furniture.
Right: View of the Drawing Room with Blüthner piano.

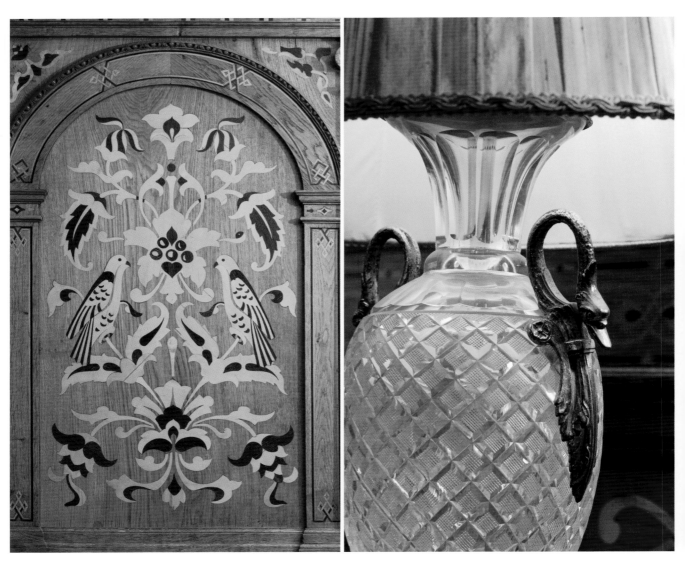

Above: Detail of inlaid wood panelling.

Above: French glass and ormolu lamp, *c.* 1920.

Above: Detail of ormolu candlestick.

Above right: Hever Castle stationery.

The Dining Hall

This splendid room was the Great Hall during the Bullens' time. It was originally open to the roof rafters but, in 1506, Thomas Bullen added a Long Gallery above it. The Bullen family would have dined here and entertained Henry VIII and his retinue when he visited. One of the impressive gilt locks on the doors in this room belonged to Henry VIII; the other is a replica. Henry VIII was worried about assassination so, to ensure his safety when visiting other houses, he brought his personal locksmith to fix a special door lock to his bedchamber.

William Waldorf Astor restored and enhanced the hall by commissioning Nathaniel Hitch to install the linenfold panelling and elaborately carved Minstrels' Gallery which, fittingly, rests on a series of carved musicians. The impressive fireplace is of Clipsham stone from Rutland, and is surmounted by the Bullen coat of arms.

The paintings are of Henry V and the Black Prince by Benjamin Burnell (*fl.* 1790–1828). Henry V (r. 1413–22) was victor of the Battle of Agincourt in 1415, during the Hundred Years War, and gained both France and the French princess, Catherine of Valois, as his wife. The Black Prince, Edward, Prince of Wales (1330–76),

was a commander during the war with victories at the Battles of Crécy and Poitiers.

The large tapestry is a detail of August from a series entitled *Months and Seasons* and was woven in Brussels in about 1540. Such tapestries would have taken many years to make and would have been very expensive.

The buffet standing at the back of the room is oak and dates from the 17th century. The coloured glass bottles and decanters date from the 19th century.

The Dining Hall, with its beautiful table and chairs, is still used for private and corporate functions. The 24 walnut armchairs which are mid 17th-century style Flemish, were reupholstered in keeping with their original design in 2000. The chairs surround the 17-ft (5.2-m) oak table, which dates from around 1600, although its top is a 20th-century replacement.

The ornate carving at Hever is one of its greatest glories – from the simple to the elaborate, all the work has been executed by craftsmen who were masters of their art, whether in Tudor times or in the 20th century.

Above: Detail of the Bullen coat of arms carved on the fireplace.

Top: Detail of Brussels tapestry depicting the months and seasons.
Above: *The Yule Log* by Robert Alexander Hillingford (1825–1904).

Above: Clipsham stone fireplace.

19

The Entrance Hall

This Entrance Hall was added to the Tudor manor house in 1506 by Thomas Bullen. Timbers dating from the late 15th century can be seen in the earlier doorway, which is directly opposite the current entrance.

Interesting furniture housed here includes an oak bench table (*c.* 1610), which would have been used by monks in their tiny cells, as well as the magnificent choir stall (*c.* 1480) which is Italian and made from walnut. There is also a caquetoire, or conversation chair, dating from the 16th century. The seat was made broad enough to accommodate wide dresses so that the ladies could chat in comfort.

The long refectory table (*c.* 1565) is Italian, and the two large vases standing on it are Japanese Imari porcelain from about 1780. The collection of dishes and plates date from 1650 to 1800.

The large leather and iron jackboots towards the end of the hall are postilions' boots and date from about 1690. A postilion was a man who rode one of a pair of horses that pulled the coach. It could be very dangerous if a leg became caught between the two horses, so each postilion wore one boot on that leg to protect himself from injury.

Above left: German tin-glazed plate, *c.* 1705.
Above: Postilions' boots, *c.* 1690.
Facing page: The Entrance Hall.

The Library

The delightful Library, which overlooks the moat and Anne Boleyn's orchard, originally contained 2,500 books, bound for William Waldorf Astor in calf and Moroccan leather, and gilt-tooled with his coat of arms. Many of these books were printed on private presses in Paris and New York during the 17th, 18th and 19th centuries. The bookcases are inspired by those owned by the diarist, Samuel Pepys.

This room was probably an estate office in Tudor times and William Waldorf Astor tried to recreate a sense of its history when he chose it as his library. The ceiling is copied from Hampton Court Palace. The carvings are in the style of Grinling Gibbons and made from a wood called sabicu, which is harder than ebony and dense enough to sink in water. The circular mahogany 'drum' table dates from around 1820 and, above the fireplace, is a portrait of Johann Jakob Astor, great-grandfather of William Waldorf Astor, and founder of the family's fortune in the late 18th century.

Left: Tunbridge ware writing slope, c. 1860. Facing page: Detail of books in the Library.

There are many examples of locally produced Tunbridge ware in the Library, including bookends, a sewing box, tea caddies and a writing slope. They all have pictures of Hever Castle as their decoration. They are made with a tessellated mosaic technique, which gives the appearance of a true mosaic, but enables intricate designs such as birds, and even pictures and portraits, to be relatively easily produced. It involves assembling slips of wood in bundles, following patterns drawn on squared papers. These are then glued and sliced transversely and reassembled into secondary blocks, which can be cut into a series of identical veneers and applied to the item being produced. Tunbridge ware became a popular choice of souvenir for wealthy tourists, peaking in popularity in the 19th century when even the young Princess Victoria purchased some as gifts.

Above: Derby-style figures depicting spring and summer, *c.* 1880.

Above: Detail of the Astor family's book collection.

Above: View of the Library showing the bust of Christopher Columbus in the foreground.

The Morning Room

The Morning Room was a private retiring room in Tudor times. The panelling and contents in this room date mainly from the 17th century. In the stone of the fireplace surround are carved the initials H.W., representing Henry Waldegrave, another of Hever's owners.

During the reign of Elizabeth I the Catholic Waldegrave family made an interesting addition to this room: it was forbidden to say Mass, so the family would have been in danger if they were caught with a Catholic priest on the premises. A 'priest hole' was incorporated into this corner of the Castle (where the china cupboard is now) in which the priest could hide. One of the many ghostly tales surrounding Hever suggests that one such priest perished here and that his unhappy spirit still lingers.

On display are several items that may have been used or worked by ladies in the 18th and 19th centuries. These include a spinning wheel (c. 1800) made of cherry wood, with ivory finials and box wood and holly inlays, and a fruit wood wool winder (c. 1825).

There are also some fine examples of needlework, including a mahogany pole fire screen (c. 1725), decorated with a needlework panel in gros and petit point. Fire screens were used as protection from the direct heat of the fire and were very popular among ladies as they prevented their complexions from becoming flushed. On the wall is a mirror which features needlework called stumpwork, depicting figures of Charles II and Catherine of Braganza, as well as animals and insects, enriched with seed pearls and gold thread. It has an original walnut frame and the raised and padded style was very fashionable between the 1630s and the 1680s.

Three-legged chairs were popular in the 17th century as they offered more stability on the extremely uneven floors. The chairs in the Morning Room date from 1620, 1625 and 1700.

Above: The Morning Room with its finely carved fireplace.
Facing page: Stumpwork mirror, c. 1684.

Anne Boleyn's Bedroom

The first room on the upper floor is a small, simple bedroom with an original 15th-century half-domed ceiling. This room is traditionally thought to have been Anne Boleyn's childhood bedroom. She may also have shared it with her sister, Mary. Anne was probably born in around 1501 but, like many children (especially girls) her birth was not recorded. She certainly spent her childhood here; the Castle had been the Bullen family home since her great-grandfather, Geoffrey, bought both Hever and Blickling Hall in Norfolk, having risen from humble beginnings to become Lord Mayor of London in 1459.

Geoffrey's grandson, Thomas, (b. 1477), brought Hever to the centre of the international stage when, in 1498, he married Elizabeth Howard, daughter of the Duke of Norfolk. This was an advantageous match, which made his three surviving children, George, Mary and Anne, related to royalty on their mother's side.

The painting in this bedroom shows Anne wearing her famous 'B' pendant and a daring French-style hood revealing her dark hair. She was intelligent and witty, if not traditionally beautiful and the Venetian ambassador said of her: '...not one of the handsomest women in the world. She is of middling stature, with a swarthy complexion, long neck, wide mouth, bosom not much raised, and in fact has nothing but the King's great appetite, and her eyes, which are black and beautiful'. Against the wall stands a bedhead with the words 'Part of Anne Boleyn's bed from Hever 1520' carved on it. It is one of the earliest Anne Boleyn 'made-up pieces' – none of it seems to date before 1600 and it was probably put together in Victorian times when there was a revival of interest in Anne Boleyn.

Top: Tudor Rose, detail from the fireplace.
Above: Detail from Anne Boleyn's bedhead.
Facing page: Portrait of Anne Boleyn, entitled *Regina Anglie, 1534*.

Henry VIII and Anne Boleyn

I n 1509, eight years after Anne Boleyn's birth, Henry Tudor, then aged 18, succeeded to the throne of England as Henry VIII. He secretly married Catherine of Aragon, the 24 year-old widow of his elder brother, Arthur. Their marriage produced only one child out of eight pregnancies; a daughter, who became the future Queen Mary I.

Anne Bullen spent much of her time as a child at Court, pushed forward by her ambitious father, Thomas. At the age of 13 she joined the household of Margaret of Austria in the Netherlands before becoming maid-of-honour to Henry's sister, Mary Tudor, who was to marry King Louis XII. Anne then became maid-of-honour to Queen Claude of France and stayed with her for nearly seven years. It was in France that Anne Bullen became known as Boleyn. There were no set spellings in Tudor times as few people could read or write, so Anne chose to sign herself Boleyn, probably from the more sophisticated sounding French pronunciation.

In 1522 Anne returned to England. Her sister, Mary, had previously been sent home in disgrace. It was rumoured she had had affairs; most notoriously, with Francis I, King of France. Soon after her return

to England, Mary became mistress to Henry VIII. Anne was by now a sophisticated young woman who had spent nine years at the most splendid and exciting Court in Europe and she found Hever quite dull in comparison. She was soon appointed lady-in-waiting to Queen Catherine, during which time she fell in love with the young Lord Henry Percy. This did not please Henry, who had other plans, so she was banished to Hever; lovesick and furious.

By 1525 King Henry was desperate for a male heir. Bored with his former mistress, Mary, he fixed his attentions on 25 year-old Anne and began to make frequent visits to Hever.

Anne was striking to look at; intelligent, sophisticated and fashionable. By that time, Henry was 32 years old, over 6 ft (1.8 m) tall, handsome, extremely athletic and well educated. Despite a relentless courtship, Anne refused to be his mistress, saying: 'Your wife I cannot be, because you have a Queen already. Your mistress I will not be', thus forcing Henry to take action in order to be able to marry her. As a Catholic, Henry had to seek the approval of the Pope to divorce Catherine. Henry was furious when the Roman Catholic Church refused his petition; thwarting his plans. He then announced that his marriage had not been legal in the first place, due to Catherine's previous marriage to Henry's brother, Arthur. Declaring himself head of the Church of England, he married Anne in secret and pronounced his marriage to Catherine null and void. Many years of religious upheaval followed his dramatic actions;

monasteries were dissolved, English Catholics rose up against the King and prominent men refused to take an oath of allegiance to Henry. Thus, the Reformation was set in motion – all for the love of Anne Boleyn from Hever.

When the pregnant Anne was crowned Queen in London in June 1533, there were few cheers. Her child, a girl, was born in September, and named Elizabeth. Anne went on to miscarry in 1534 and again in 1536. Henry began to believe that this marriage was cursed and Anne's lady-in-waiting, Jane Seymour, was moved into new quarters at Henry's palace. By May 1536, Anne was a prisoner in the Tower of London, accused of incest with her brother, adultery with several gentlemen from Court, witchcraft and treason. She was found guilty and sentenced to death by burning; but her sentence was commuted to beheading. She was buried in the Chapel of St Peter ad Vincula in the Tower of London. Her father, his world in ruins, died two years later and was buried in St Peter's Church, Hever.

Although Anne only reigned for 1,000 days and failed to provide Henry with a male heir, it was her daughter, Elizabeth I, who became one of the longest-reigning monarchs that England has ever had. After Anne was executed, Henry promptly married Jane Seymour, who later died in childbirth.

Top left and right: Portrait of Henry VIII, *c.* 1535, Anglo Flemish workshop.
Portrait of Anne Boleyn, *c.* 1550, English School.

In 1540 Henry married again, this time to Anne of Cleves, the daughter of a German duke. The marriage was agreed for political reasons and on the strength of a flattering miniature portrait by Court painter Hans Holbein. The marriage was annulled after six months and 'the Flanders Mare', as she was nicknamed, was given Hever Castle as part of the divorce settlement.

❛ **And thus I take my leave of the world and of you all, and I heartily desire you all to pray for me. O Lord have mercy on me, to God I commend my soul. O Lord have mercy on me, to God I commend my soul. O Lord have mercy on me...** ❜

Anne Boleyn's reported final words.

The 'Book of Hours' Room

The two beautifully illuminated prayer books on display belonged to Anne. She wrote in them and they bear her signature. These personal prayer books were popular in England from the 13th century until the Reformation and earned the name 'Book of Hours' from the short services to the Virgin Mary which were read at eight fixed hours during the day – including Matins and Vespers.

These books also contained a calendar of church festivals, psalms, prayers, favourite saints and services for the dead. The earliest one on display was handwritten on vellum in Bruges, *c.* 1450, and bears the poignant inscription *Le temps viendra* (The time will come), *Je Anne Boleyn.* The other is believed to be the prayer book Anne took with her to her execution at the Tower and bears the following inscription.

❛ **Remember me when you do pray that hope doth lead from day to day. Anne Boleyn .** ❜

'Book of Hours', *c.* 1528

The large tapestry illustrates the marriage of Princess Mary Rose (sister of Henry VIII) to Louis XII of France in 1514. Anne Boleyn and her sister Mary may be among the ladies depicted in the tapestry as they were present at the wedding. Princess Mary was 18, while Louis was 52 and died three months after the marriage. Princess Mary then married her sweetheart, Charles Brandon, Duke of Suffolk. Their daughter, Frances, was Lady Jane Grey's mother.

Top: View of the 'Book of Hours' Room.
Right: Detail from an illustrated border in the 1450 'Book of Hours'.
Facing page: Miniature depicting the Adoration of the Magi in the 1450 'Book of Hours'.

Ens in Ad sextam.
aditutorium meum
intende. Domine ad ad
iuuandum me festina.

The Queens' Chamber

1 Portrait of **Catherine of Aragon**, 16th-century English School. Divorced. Catherine of Aragon (1485–1536), Henry's first and longest reigning Queen had previously been married at the age of 16 to Henry's older brother, Arthur. After many pregnancies, the only surviving child from her marriage to Henry was a girl, Mary. Catherine, a devout Catholic, refused to accept her subsequent divorce from Henry and so was forced to live in humble conditions and apart from her daughter until she died. Her acceptance never came and, before she died at the age of 50, she signed her last letter 'Catherine the Queen'.

2 Portrait of **Anne Boleyn**, c. 1550, holding a red rose. Beheaded. Anne Boleyn (1501–36), Queen for 1,000 days, whose story is told in this guidebook.

3 Portrait of **Jane Seymour**, 16th century, after Holbein. Died. Jane Seymour (1507/8?–37) was lady-in-waiting to Anne Boleyn; she became engaged to Henry the day after Anne's execution and married him ten days later. She gave birth to a son, the future King Edward VI but died of complications shortly afterwards. Henry's wish was to be buried next to Jane when he died.

4 Portrait of **Anne of Cleves**, 16th century, after Barthel Bruyn the Elder. Divorced. Anne of Cleves (1515–57), the daughter of a German duke, who Henry married for political reasons and on the basis of a miniature portrait by the Court painter, Holbein. When the pair met, however, Henry was shocked at how Anne really looked and by her lack of education. It was too late to cancel the marriage but Henry had it annulled after six months. Anne was given Hever Castle as part of the divorce settlement and eventually enjoyed a happy, platonic relationship with the King who called her 'sister'.

5 Portrait of **Catherine Howard**, 16th century, follower of Holbein. Beheaded. Catherine Howard (1521?–42) was Anne Boleyn's cousin and came to Court as a lady-in-waiting to Anne of Cleves. She was sentenced to death for treason and was beheaded at the Tower of London. Her reported final words were 'I die a Queen but I would rather have died the wife of Culpepper,' Culpepper being the name of one of her lovers.

6 Portrait of **Catherine Parr**, *c.* 1528, English School. Survived. Catherine Parr (1512–48), had been married and widowed twice before and had just begun a romance with Thomas Seymour, Jane Seymour's brother, when Henry took a liking to her. When Henry died only four years later, Catherine married her old love, Thomas Seymour. By then she was in her mid thirties and had no children, despite four marriages. She finally fell pregnant, but died the following year from complications.

Rare portrait of Prince Arthur, *c*. 1500. Arthur was the older brother of Henry VIII. Arthur's early death changed the course of history: as the eldest it was he who had been heir to the throne.

The Tudors

| ARTHUR Prince of Wales (d. 1502) | = | CATHERINE of Aragon | **HENRY VIII** r. 1509–47 | = | (1) CATHERINE of Aragon (d. 1536) daughter of Ferdinand V, first King of Spain and widow of Arthur, Prince of Wales. Divorced 1533. | = | (2) ANNE daughter of Thomas Boleyn, Earl of Wiltshire. Executed 1536 | = | (3) JANE (d. 1537) daughter of Sir John Seymour of Wolf Hall, Wiltshire | = | (4) ANNE (d. 1557) daughter of John, Duke of Cleves. Divorced 1540. |

| **MARY I** r. 1553–58 | = | PHILIP II King of Spain, son of Emperor Charles V | | **ELIZABETH I** r. 1558–1603 | | **EDWARD VI** r. 1547–53 |

Edward VI

JAMES I (James VI, King of Scotland, 1567–1625, who became first Sovereign in England of the House of Stuart, 1603)

Portrait of Henry VIII, *c*. 1535, Anglo-Flemish workshop. Henry VIII (r. 1509–47) is probably England's best-known monarch, famous for his bloodthirsty actions and for having six wives. Many of his actions were an attempt to secure a Tudor male heir to the throne. His desperation came as hs own claim to the throne was tenuous, it having been taken by force by his father and, historically, no female monarch had ever successfully reigned in her own right.

Mary I

Portrait of Elizabeth I, 1558, English School

Henry VII

Lady MARGARET BEAUFORT = (1) EDMUND TUDOR
Earl of Richmond, son of Owen Tudor
by Catherine, widow of King Henry V
   (2) SIR HENRY STAFFORD
   (3) THOMAS STANLEY
Lord Stanley became 1st Earl of Derby

HENRY VII = ELIZABETH OF YORK
r. 1485–1509 (d. 1503) daughter of Edward IV

Elizabeth
of York

= (5) CATHERINE
daughter of
Lord Edmund
Howard.
Executed 1542.

= (6) CATHERINE
(d. 1548) daughter of Sir Thomas Parr
of Kendal, and widow of Sir Edward
Borough, and John Nevill, Lord Latymer.
After Henry VIII died she married
Thomas, Lord Seymour of Sudeley.

MARGARET = (1) JAMES IV
King of Scotland
   (2) ARCHIBALD DOUGLAS
   6th Earl of Angus
    (divorced 1527)
    (3) HENRY STUART Lord Methven

Mary = (1) LOUIS XII
(d. 1533) (2) CHARLES
BRANDON,
Duke of Suffolk

JAMES V
King of Scotland
1513–42

= (1) MADELINE
(d. 1537) daughter of Francis I,
King of France
(2) MARY of Lorraine (d. 1560)
daughter of Claude, Duke of Guise

MARGARET = MATTHEW STUART
(d. 1578) 4th Earl of Lennox

HENRY
Earl of Lincoln

FRANCES = (1) HENRY GREY
(d. 1559) Duke of Suffolk,
executed 1554
   (2) ADRIAN
   STOKES

MARY
Queen of Scots
(executed 1587)

= (1) FRANCIS,
Dauphin of France,
afterwards Francis II

= (2) HENRY STUART
Lord Darnley,
murdered 1587

= (3) JAMES HEPBURN
Earl of Bothwell

CHARLES STUART = ELIZABETH
6th Earl of Lennox daughter of
Sir William
Cavendish

Lady JANE GREY = GUILDFORD DUDLEY
Queen, July 1553
(executed 1554)

Lady CATHERINE GREY = EDWARD SEYMOUR
Earl of Hertford

Lady MARY GREY = THOMAS
(d. 1578) KEYES

EDWARD SEYMOUR = HONORA
Lord Beauchamp (d. 1612) daughter of Sir Richard Rogers

THOMAS SEYMOUR = ISABEL ONLEY
(d. 1600)

(1) Lady ARABELLA STUART = WILLIAM SEYMOUR
(d. 1615) Duke of Somerset, (d.1660)

= (2) FRANCES
daughter of Robert Devereux, Earl of Sussex

from whom descends HM Queen Elizabeth The Queen Mother (deceased)

The Staircase Gallery

The Staircase Gallery is the smaller of the two galleries in the Castle and was created in 1506 by Thomas Bullen over the Entrance Hall to give access between the two wings of the house and his newly built Long Gallery upstairs.

Along this gallery there are two impressive portraits of Anne Boleyn's daughter Elizabeth I (r. 1558-1603). Elizabeth was the last Tudor monarch and, as she never married, succession then passed to James I (VI of Scotland), son of Mary, Queen of Scots.

The delightful baby clothes in the cabinet are complemented by a panelled oak cradle with a domed canopy and child's high chair that date to around 1625. There is also a collection of items purchased from Ashridge House, Hertfordshire, including 17th-century personal possessions in embroidered silk, such as indoor slippers, brushes, a night cap, purse and comb case.

Left: View of the Staircase Gallery.

King Henry VIII's Bedchamber

Although Henry VIII visited the castle, it is impossible to know for certain in which room he slept. However, this is one of the largest bedchambers in the Castle and was restored by the Astor family to be fit for a King of Henry's importance and proportions. It is true to say that the Castle's best rooms would have been prepared for the King, and hosting him and his retinue would have been a large burden for any household; particularly for a relatively small one like Hever.

Above: French toilet mirror, c. 1700.
Facing page: View of Henry VIII's bedchamber showing the tester bed made of finely carved oak, c. 1540.

The magnificent bed in this room, with its blue velvet hangings, is certainly the type that the monarch would be used to. It dates from 1540 and is a 'tester' bed, named after the solid wooden canopy suspended above it. By the fire hangs a Dutch brass warming-pan dating from the 18th century, which would have been used as an early form of bed heating in an otherwise cold and draughty Castle. The pan would have been filled with hot embers from the fire and placed under the bedclothes to heat and air the bed. The earliest known example of a warming pan was made in 1616.

The ceiling in the bedchamber is the oldest in the Castle, dating from around 1462. The panelling dates from 1565, with the exception of the section over the fireplace, which commemorates the two wives of Henry VIII who lived at Hever Castle – Anne Boleyn and Anne of Cleves.

Above: Detail of tester bed.

Above: Detail of the fireplace.

Above: 17th-century ebonised hour-glass.

The Waldegrave Room

This room is named after the Waldegrave family, who lived at Hever through the reigns of the last of the Tudor monarchs and into the Stuart dynasty. When the Catholic Queen Mary I (eldest daughter of Henry VIII) came to the throne in 1553, the Waldegraves were in royal favour. In 1557, after the death of Anne of Cleves, Sir Edward Waldegrave was appointed one of the Commissioners to sell any land that the crown had seized, and promptly assigned the Castle to himself. It was to remain in the possession of the Waldegrave family for over 158 years; longer than any other owner of the Castle. When Queen Mary died and Elizabeth I came to the throne in 1558 the small chapel, or oratory, was built, hidden behind panelling so Sir Edward could practice his faith in secret.

In 1683, Henry Waldegrave married Henrietta FitzJames, the illegitimate daughter of James, Duke of York, pictured in this room. With the accession to the throne of King James II, the first Catholic monarch since the days of Queen Mary, Henry's fortune seemed assured and he was created the 1st Baron Waldegrave. A future of high office seemed likely but the new wind, for which the Waldegraves had waited so long, proved fickle: the country would not accept a Catholic King. Prince William of Orange landed at Torbay and King James fled to France. Henry collected a large sum of money which he took to the King in Paris, but he died there the following year.

Henry's son, James (named after the King), had learned a long and painful lesson. Catholics were out of favour and likely to remain so, so he renounced his faith, took the Oath of Supremacy, conformed to the Church of England and took his seat in the House of Lords. It proved to be an advantageous move. He was appointed Ambassador to France in 1725 and, in 1729, was elevated to the Earldom of Waldegrave. In 1735 he became a Privy Councillor. The little castle at Hever proved too small to match his growing status, so, in 1715, he sold it to Sir William Humphreys, a former Lord Mayor of London.

The 'Rhyming Blade Sword' in the cabinet is one of only five known to exist and was created in support of the 1745 Jacobite Rebellion. Figures of James III

and various saints are engraved on each side of the blade and it bears the inscription: 'With this sword thy cause I will maintain; And for they sack (sake) O James breath (break) each vein.'

Left: Carving detail in the Oratory.
Facing page: The Waldegrave Room, with its French oak and walnut four-poster bed, c. 1485.

Above: Italian rock crystal cross, *c.* 1700.

Above: Detail of chest panel depicting scenes from *The Book of Genesis, c.* 1505.

Above: Italian rock crystal reliquary cross, c. 1800.

Above: The Oratory Chapel with its 19th-century painting of *The Virgin in Ecstasy* above the Spanish altar.

The Long Gallery

The Long Gallery is more than 98 ft (30 m) long and runs the entire width of the building. The Long Gallery is an architectural term given to a long narrow room, often with a high ceiling, usually located on the upper floor of the great houses of the time. This one was created in 1506 by Thomas Bullen, who put a ceiling over the Great Hall below. The Long Gallery served several purposes: it was used for entertaining guests, for taking exercise when the weather was inclement, and for displaying art collections. Tradition has it that Henry VIII held Court in the alcove at the far end of the Long Gallery when he visited the Castle.

The panelling in the gallery is Elizabethan and the ceiling is a 16th century-style reproduction made for William Waldorf Astor.

The four beautiful chandeliers are copies of originals at Hampton Court Palace and the stained glass in the windows shows the coats of arms of successive owners of the Castle. The views from the Long Gallery include, from the east windows, the Tudor gardens and topiary cut to the shape of a medieval-style chess set and from the west windows Anne Boleyn's Orchard, which is a riot of yellow daffodils in the spring.

The coats of arms in the stained glass commemorate the different owners of Hever Castle since it was built. They include, at the west end, the coat of arms of Sir John Fastolf, who owned the Castle from 1408 to 1423. Fastolf was later characterised as Falstaff by William Shakespeare in *Henry IV (Parts I* and *II), Henry V* and *The Merry Wives of Windsor*.

' Hever Castle, once the home of that great figure of Tudor history, Anne Boleyn, now has one of the best collections of Tudor portraits after the National Portrait Gallery. '

David Starkey

Facing page: View of the Long Gallery.
Right: Detail of stained glass window and ornate plasterwork.

Clockwise from top left: Anne of Cleves; Sir William Humphreys and Sir Timothy Waldo;
John de Cobham; William de Hever; Sir Stephen Scrope and Sir John Fastolf; Anne Boleyn;
James, 2nd Baron Waldegrave.

Clockwise from above: Henry VIII; George Medley; James Fiennes; Edmund G.B. Meade Waldo.

The Astor Suite

This section of the Castle is dedicated to its more recent history. It contains pictures and memorabilia relating to the Astor family, who were the owners for 80 years from 1903. This remarkable American family was responsible for most of what visitors see today. They restored, added to and enhanced the existing rooms and then searched the world for paintings, furniture, carpets, tapestries and *objets d'art* worthy of furnishing and decorating their fine home.

The Astor family's story is a 'rags to riches' one, just like that of the Bullens in Tudor times. In 1783, a butcher's boy called Johann Jakob Astor emigrated from the small German town of Walldorf to America. He took up fur-trading in the north-east,

buying his furs from the Indian trappers. He became more and more successful until, by the end of the 18th century, he owned a fleet of 12 merchant vessels. which carried his furs to Europe and the Far East and returned with manufactured goods and tea, which he sold in America. His main base for trading was in the state of Oregon, later to be renamed Astoria in his honour. Astor was a shrewd investor in New York real estate and, when he died in 1848, he was the richest man in America. Succeeding generations extended the family interests in politics, hotels, magazines, newspapers, racehorses and agriculture.

Hever Castle was restored by William Waldorf Astor, Johann Jakob Astor's great-grandson, with all the comforts of Edwardian life in mind. It has bathrooms with modern plumbing, electricity and central heating but it is hard to spot light switches, radiators or pipes, as many are carefully concealed.

William Waldorf Astor inherited the benefits of the original fortune and the continuing success in business and investment of the next two generations. He also developed a love for Europe, particularly when he was appointed American Ambassador to Italy between 1882 and 1885. He grew increasingly disenchanted with his native land, however, and announced publicly that 'America was no longer a fit place for a gentleman to live.' He left America for England in 1890 with a reputed 100 million dollars (the equivalent of at least ten times that amount today) and totally absorbed

Left: The Astor Suite, with family memorabilia.
Facing page: Ledger belonging to John Jacob Astor,
1st Baron Astor of Hever.

MAJOR THE HONBLE J. J. ASTOR

PERSONAL LEDGER

No 3

Above: Walnut bureau, c. 1695, with family photos.

Above: Portrait of John Jacob Astor,
1st Baron Astor of Hever.

himself in his adopted country, buying Cliveden in Buckinghamshire in 1893 and, ten years later, Hever Castle and 640 acres of land from the Meade Waldo family.

At Hever, Astor was able to translate his historical sense and romantic taste into his own 'grand design'. He was a man of enormous energy and vision: he wanted to live in 20th-century style and comfort and to entertain lavishly but, at the same time, preserve the Castle itself and to perpetuate its historical associations.

Between 1903 and 1908, with his architect, F.L. Pearson, Astor set about building a complete 100-room wing in the style of a Tudor village, on the far side of the Castle moat, joining the two parts with a covered bridge. The village-style wing was designed so that it could be kept to a scale that allowed the Castle to remain the dominant building, so the apparently separate cottages were constructed of varying materials, shapes, angles and styles within the whole Tudor concept but, inside the structure, all the rooms were joined by corridors and service areas to provide sumptuous rooms for family and guests.

Cellars were built underneath the Astor Wing, as this annexe is now known, and also part of the Castle. Enormous boilers to provide hot water and central heating were installed in them. Miles of cables and pipes running through these cellars provide power, light, heat and water to the entire complex. Astor also had a fire-fighting system, a power station and a private water supply.

Astor's massive project employed an incredible 748 craftsmen, including the most skilled plasterers, carpenters, stonemasons and metal workers of their generation, and Astor visited many Tudor and Elizabethan buildings for inspiration. In order to achieve the final design, the bed of the River Eden and the nearby public road had to be moved to create sufficient room for the village. The lake and gardens were also created; the work largely carried out by hand with a further workforce of 800 men.

In 1916 Astor was created Baron and, in 1917, Viscount Astor. He died in 1919 and was succeeded by his elder son, Waldorf, who had been born in 1879 and educated in England. In 1905, Waldorf married the celebrated and formidable Nancy Langhorne from Virginia who famously disliked Winston Churchill, and who, as Lady Nancy Astor, was the first woman to take her seat in the House of Commons.

Astor's younger son, John Jacob V, succeeded to the ownership of Hever in 1918 after distinguished service in the Life Guards during World War I. He was MP for Dover from 1922 to 1945 and continued his father's charitable and business interests. He was elevated to the peerage in 1956 as 1st Baron Astor of Hever, and the two titles remain in the family today. He was, in turn, succeeded by Gavin, 2nd Baron of Hever, who also served in the Life Guards in World War II and later devoted his energies to the newspaper world as Chairman of the Board of The Times Publishing Company and, later, Life President of Times Newspapers Ltd.

He also carried out further improvements to the Astor Wing and in 1963 he opened the Castle and gardens to the public for the first time. Gavin was succeeded by his eldest son, John Jacob VIII, 3rd Baron Astor, in 1984.

Throughout the Astor family's association with Hever, it remained a comfortable family home, albeit a lavish one, where they could live and entertain their many guests. The homeliness is nowhere better seen than in the three small bedrooms in the Astor Suite corridor which were created in 1968 for the three daughters of the house. Each was allowed to choose their own dècor and the rooms were affectionately known as the 'Dog Kennels' by the Astors.

These bedrooms were created following a disastrous event in the Castle's more recent history, one that nearly obliterated much of the Astor's restoration work on the ground floor and the collections that had been lovingly gathered by them in the preceding decades. The Castle had

been flooded in 1958, but a severe storm on 15 September 1968 caused more than 5 in (12.5 cm) of rain to fall in 16 hours. Hever is situated close to the River Eden (a tributary of the Medway) and only 117.5 ft (36 m) above sea level. Consequently, water poured through about 100 rooms of the Castle and the neighbouring Astor Wing and six cottages and stables, to a depth of 4.5 ft (1.4 m). The flooding began at about 10.30 am and by 6 pm members of staff and other occupants began to be taken out of the buildings by boat and lifeline. By 9 pm the rescue was complete but the Castle's contents on the ground floor were completely ruined; some had to be destroyed on health grounds and some were sent to be restored. The walls and floors were not dried out enough to permit redecoration and refurnishing until 1970 and renovation work was not completed until 1972.

It seems that neither nature, nor history, have managed to destroy the attractive Castle that visitors enjoy today.

Since 1983, the whole property has been in the ownership of the Yorkshire-based private company, Broadland Properties Ltd.

Top: 'Dog Kennel' bedroom.
Facing page: Easel set; a present to John Jacob Astor from Winston Churchill, who lived at nearby Chartwell. Both men were keen artists.

The Gatehouse

The tour of the Castle concludes in the oldest part – the medieval Council Chamber in the Gatehouse. The first 13th-century owners of the Castle would have eaten, slept and entertained here, and it also contains the garderobe, a 13th-century toilet, which emptied directly into the moat. A raised dais with two throne-like chairs illustrates how the Lord of the Manor would have used the room for meetings and dispensing justice when it was still used as a Council Chamber.

The Gatehouse would originally have had several defence mechanisms such as a portcullis, moat, drawbridge, murder holes and machicolations, some of which are still visible. It now contains collections of historic swords and armour, as well as instruments of execution, torture and discipline, including several German beheading swords dating from the 16th and 17th centuries. An early 18th-century torture collar with deep spikes is particularly gruesome. There is also a cast-iron mantrap from around 1800 which was used to catch trespassers and poachers; these became illegal in 1861.

The scolds' bridles – also called branks – were designed for outspoken women who defied authority and were public nuisances. Bridles prevented them from speaking; some had a tongue plate formed from a flat piece of iron that prevented tongue movement, while others had a spiked iron bit.

The exit stairs are a defensive spiral staircase and will take you back into the Castle Courtyard where the difference in age between the 13th-century Gatehouse and timber-framed Tudor additions is most obvious. The front portcullis is said to be one of the oldest working portcullises in the country. The drawbridge was reinstated by William Waldorf Astor and can still be raised.

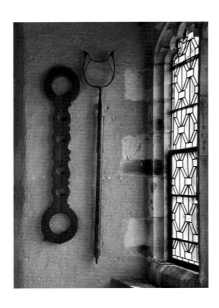

Left: Wooden neck halter and jailer's neck trap.
Above: Scold's bridle.
Facing page: The portcullis.

The Gardens

The Gardens

The beautiful gardens at Hever Castle were laid out between 1904 and 1908 by Joseph Cheal and Son, turning marshland into the spectacular gardens you see today, which are a pleasure to visit at any time of the year.

One of the most magnificent areas of the gardens is the Italian Garden, which was designed to display William Waldorf Astor's collection of Italian sculpture. Over 1,000 men worked on the grand design with around 800 men taking two years to dig out the 38-acre (14.2 ha) lake at the far end of the Italian Garden. Within four years the 125 acres (50 ha) of classical and natural landscapes were constructed and planted. The garden is only now reaching its full maturity and includes the colourful walled Rose Garden which contains over 4,000 bushes.

There are many water features around the gardens, including Half Moon Pond, the Cascade, the cool and shady grottoes, the formal Loggia fountain inspired by the Trevi fountain in Rome, and the less formal Two Sisters' Pond.

Other areas that you can stroll through include the Tudor Garden, Rhododendron Walk and Anne Boleyn's Walk, with its collection of trees planted more than 100 years ago.

In recent years, the present owners have made several changes to the gardens, including the installation of the Millennium Fountain that can be found on Sixteen Acre Island forming an interesting feature at the far end of this more informal area of the gardens. The 100-metre herbaceous border has been reinstated and Sunday Walk created, providing a peaceful woodland garden following the course of a stream. In addition to the existing Yew Maze, a splashing Water Maze has been built on Sixteen Acre Island – a unique feature which is especially popular with children.

With over 20,000 spring bulbs planted in the gardens each year, visitors are guaranteed a breath-taking display.

Spring

Spring is a wonderful time to view the gardens at Hever Castle: a carpet of thousands of yellow and cream daffodils welcomes visitors in Anne Boleyn's Orchard and surrounding areas. There are

also spectacular swathes of spring bulbs to see, such as dainty snowdrops (*Galanthus*), purple crocuses, elegant scilla, vigorous little grape hyacinths (*Muscari*), low growing *Choinodoxa* and vivid bluebells (*Hyacinthoides non-scripta*).

Left: *Galanthus*, the snowdrop, bordering the castle's outer moat.
Facing page: View from the Blue Garden.

The spring borders are a delight to the eye, with an impressive palette of colours created by the rhododendrons, azaleas, acers and mock-orange (*Philadelphus*). In the Italian Garden primulas, violas, wallflowers and tulips of every shape and hue create a dazzling display. This is also the time of the year that the first flowering clematis, *Clematis armandii*, begins to produce its exquisite, white flowers, which smell almost honey-like, against the backdrop of long, evergreen leaves.

Do not miss the wonderful Yew Maze, which has more than 1,000 individual yew trees lining its winding paths.

The gardens at Hever offer more than just a visual display – all senses are stimulated as wonderful scents waft in the air, spring breezes rustle freshly formed foliage and the drooping heads of lilac wisteria blooms. As spring progresses, the sweet scent of the golden flowers of the *Rhododendron luteum* fills the air. In the Blue Garden fragrant, deep blue, full heads of the 'King of the Blues' hyacinth (*Hyacinthus orientalis*) emerge.

In late spring the walls of the Pergola Walk are bedecked with an array of different varieties of camellia, including *Camellia sinensis*, commonly known as the tea plant whose leaves create the nation's favourite drink.

More than 15,000 bedding plants are planted in the gardens annually, ensuring a wonderful display, no matter what weather conditions the seasons bring.

The Hever Castle Rose is a new addition to the gardens launched by Dame Judi Dench, the award-winning actress. With its wonderful velvety deep-red blooms, golden-yellow stamens and resistance to disease, this rose is proving extremely popular.

Top: Golden Stairs.
Above: Italian Garden.

Above: West face of the castle from Topiary Walk.

Above: Looking towards the Castle from Rhododendron Walk.

Above: Meandering steps in the Blue Garden.

Top: Spring Border from the Half Moon Pond.
Above: Spring bedding in the Italian Garden.

Above right: Large earthenware jar, about 2,000 years old,
once used for storing olive oil, milk or water.

Summer

Nothing is more quintessentially English than a rose garden in full bloom, and the roses at Hever are particularly admired, with more than 4,000 beautifully displayed bushes creating a kaleidoscope of colour and wonderfully perfumed aromas. There is an endless variety of roses in the gardens, but especially look out for a purplish, highly perfumed rose, 'Rhapsody in Blue', and the large blowsy 'Buxom Beauty', as well as the numerous *Rosa floribunda* varieties and dramatic climbing roses. The Tudor Garden features billowing pale pink *Rosa* 'Ballerina', while at Half Moon Pond enjoy the dark red, velvety petals of *Rosa* 'Deep Secret'.

The Rose Bank on Two Sisters' Lawn is also a delight with the musky fragrances of gallica, bourbon, musk and damask roses together with a rare collection of Gold Standard Award roses.

As the days lengthen, the Mediterranean-style planting within the Pompeiian Wall bursts into life with exotic treats such as olives, kiwis, figs and pomegranates, all brimming with fruit. Look up and see the horse chestnut trees with their elevated pink and white blossom heads forming an elegant backdrop to the variety of colours and shapes that greet visitors at eye level.

Facing page: The Pompeiian wall.

Top: Sunken Garden.
Above: View in the Italian Gardens.

The herbaceous border at Hever has been designed in a Gertrude Jekyll style and displays hundreds of different perennials, each vying for attention. Notice how the colours move from silver and white to blue, purple, pink and then yellow, orange and red at the centre, before falling back through these colours to silver and white again.

As summer progresses and then begins to fade, more than 400 dahlias begin to create their own dazzling displays of colour at Two Sisters' Lawn, presenting an uplifting vista right through until the first frosts of autumn appear.

The Herb Garden, which forms part of the Tudor Garden, also looks at its best in summer.

The gardens at Hever are award-winning and both the gardens and Castle have been used as television and film sets.

Autumn

Autumn is the season in which Hever's striking trees come to the fore, with the yellow, red and orange leaves of beech (*Fagus*), liquid amber (*Liquidamber styraciflua*) and Japanese maples (*Acer*) all contributing to an explosion of colour. Other trees and shrubs seem to compete by revealing beautifully coloured bark and stems that exhibit stunning autumnal colours.

Top: The Herbaceous Border.
Centre left: An amphora nestling amongst red valerian (*Centranthus ruber*).
Centre right and above: The Rose Garden.

Above: A profusion of Ballerina shrub roses within the Tudor Garden.

Above: Millennium Fountain.

Top: The Dahlia Border.
Above: Boating on the lake overlooking the
Loggia and Piazza.

View of the lake at sunrise from the Loggia.

Top: Outer moat.
Above: Anne Boleyn's Walk.

The Nymph's Fountain made by W.S. Frith in 1908, inspired by the Trevi Fountain in Rome.

Top: Autumnal fruits.
Above: Golden yew 'chess set' in the Tudor Garden.

Above: Looking towards the Castle from the
Rhododendron Walk.

The spectacular Boston ivy (*Parthenocissus tricuspidata*) that scrambles up the Castle seems to clothe the walls in a warm, colourful coat as its leaves change from green to red, while the dazzling purple berries of the beauty berry (*Callicarpa*), and the clear blue fruits which emerge amongst the striking pink, cream and green variegated leaves of the ampelopsis offer a treat for wildlife.

Even in autumn there are usually late roses still worth seeing in the gardens and numerous vines, especially in the Italian Garden, although admittedly some of the grapes they produce are not as tasty as others! The Dahlia Border also maintains its interest throughout autumn and is complemented by the magnificent display of statuary, which creates a sense of continuity in an ever-changing scene.

Visitors strolling through the gardens may be lucky enough to catch the mouth-watering smell of the Katsura tree (*Cercidiphyllum japonicum*), which has a toffee-like or candyfloss aroma complementing the beauty of heart-shaped leaves, which are orange and pink in autumn.

The 'Great Storm' of October 1987, which swept through large parts of southern England, felled more than 1,000 trees in the gardens at Hever. Most of these, if not all, have now been replanted.

Right: The Golden Stairs.
Facing page: Piazza in the snow.

Winter

As winter approaches, the warm red bark of the redwood trees glow against the winter sky and the *Malus* and quince-like medlar fruits glisten in the frost. The last of the red and purple leaves of the magnificent crimson glory vine (*Vitis coignetiae*) fall to the floor, creating a multi-hued carpet underfoot.

The majestic hellebores nod gracefully in the winter sun and the witch hazels and viburnum begin to bloom, a sure sign that winter is drawing to a close and that spring is on the horizon.

The yew topiary stands majestically on the way up to the castle and becomes especially striking when it is tinged with frost or dusted with snow. If you are lucky enough to see it in moonlight, the silhouettes create an almost eerie presence in the gardens.

The gardens at Hever are home to an ever-changing display of wonderful plants and structures and the collection is constantly being enhanced. One fascinating recent addition is the wollemi pine (*Wollemia nobilis*), one of the oldest known tree species in the world, dating back to the time of the dinosaurs.

Much of the statuary and sculpture in the gardens is more than 2,000 years old and was collected by the Astor family in the 20th century, along with the diverse collection of trees, which includes tulip trees, handkerchief trees and Indian bean trees.

Yew topiary during winter.

Hever Hospitality

Hever Castle has played host to important events and celebrations for over 700 years. In 1903 when William Waldorf Astor set about restoring it to its former glory, he added the 'Tudor Village' to accommodate his family and guests before creating a lake and the spectacular Italian Gardens to house his impressive collection of ancient Greek and Roman statuary.

Today the Astor Wing in the 'Tudor Village' together with the Guthrie Pavilion and areas of the Castle itself are available for corporate and private events on an 'exclusive use' basis. Each venue has its own unique character and offers peace, privacy and seclusion in one of the most historic and beautiful settings in England.

The Astor Wing boasts three impressive inter-connecting rooms offering an ideal environment for meetings, conferences and presentations where delegates require peace and security combined with unobtrusive service. The recently restored Guthrie Pavilion overlooking the 38-acre lake is a fabulous new venue for meetings and corporate events where something a little different is required. The Castle's magnificent wood-panelled Tudor Suite Dining Room offers an impressive venue for private lunches or dinners. Alternatively, the Tudor Suite Sitting Room has a more intimate atmosphere ideal for smaller parties

and gatherings. Both rooms, along with the Tudor Suite Breakfast Room, are suitable for canapés and drinks receptions.

After the business of the day, delegates and guests can relax over dinner and stroll through the gardens before retiring to the Astor Wing's luxurious bedrooms. Having recently undergone a major refurbishment, the 21 individually styled en-suite rooms have a contemporary yet classic feel; all have complimentary Wi-Fi, digital flat screen TV and tea and coffee making facilities.

In addition, Medley Court, our luxury self-contained accommodation, adjoins the Astor Wing and comprises four sumptuous bedrooms, an impressive drawing room and a spacious, modern well-equipped kitchen. Ideal for either smaller parties or for larger groups in conjunction with the Astor Wing.

An outdoor heated swimming pool, all-weather tennis court, croquet lawn and billiard room are available for use, as is the Hever Castle Golf Club, a 27-hole course to challenge even the most accomplished golfer.

Depending upon availability, luxury bed and breakfast accommodation can also be booked in the Astor Wing bedrooms individually by guests looking for an overnight stay or short break.

**For further details telephone 01732 861 800
E-mail: tudor@hevercastle.co.uk
Website: www.hevercastle.co.uk**

Top: Hever Castle and the Astor Wing.
Centre and above: Two of the sumptuous bedrooms.

Above: Tudor Suite Dining Room.

Events and other attractions

Shopping The Hever shops offer a unique shopping experience for everyone, with a beautiful array of exclusive gifts, souvenirs, local produce, children's toys and a large selection of books. Estate-grown plants and shrubs can be purchased at the Courtyard Shop.

Eating Visitors will enjoy a warm and friendly welcome in the award-winning licensed Guthrie Pavilion and Moat restaurants, which serve delicious freshly cooked hot dishes, afternoon teas, sandwiches, snacks and drinks throughout the day. The restaurants are also available to hire for private celebrations.

Miniature Model Houses A unique collection of $1/12$ scale model houses, which was commissioned by the current owners of Hever Castle, from the master English miniaturist furniture maker, John J. Hodgson. The models are set in a permanent display and journey through medieval times to the Victorian age.

Adventure Playground Shaded by mature trees, children up to the age of 14 years can let off steam in the enclosed wooden playground. There is a variety of wooden climbing frames, swings, slides and the Tower Maze. Equipment for the under fives is also available.

The Yew Maze Measuring 80 by 80 ft (24.3 m by 24.3 m), the hedges are up to eight feet high with almost a quarter of a mile (0.4 km) of pathways inside. It is one of only a few traditionally designed mazes in the country.

The Water Maze Situated on Sixteen Acre Island, the maze consists of a series of concentric stepping-stone walkways sitting over water; at intervals the hidden water jets spring into action to soak the unwary visitor. Few reach the grotto in the centre without getting wet; however, it is very popular and challenges young and old alike.

Lake & Rowing Visitors can discover the local wildlife including kingfishers, swans, herons and crested grebes on the hour-long nature walk around the 38-acre (15.4 ha) lake. At the foot of the lake are the waterfall, weir and three WWII pill boxes. Traditionally built rowing boats can be hired from the boathouse.

Above: The Hever Shop.

Top and centre: Miniature Houses.
Above: Guthrie Pavilion Pergola.

Top: Yew Maze.
Above: Water Maze.

Events Hever Castle plays host to a variety of special events throughout the year, including the annual jousting tournaments with the Knights of Royal England, medieval weekends, gardening events and half-term activities.

Hever Castle Golf Club Hever is an idyllic setting for a championship 18-hole course, a 9-hole course, driving range, practice facility, large professional shop, bar, restaurant, sun terrace and function venue. It is considered to be one of the best golf courses in the area.

Photography by Peter Smith of Newbery Smith Photography Ltd and Hever Castle.
Designed and produced by Jigsaw Design & Publishing.
ISBN 978-1-917750-30-4
Printed by Swallowtail Print, Norwich, Great Britain 2012-1/12